W9-CET-976

THE SHOSHONE PEOPLE

BY KRISTEN RAJCZAK

Gareth Stevens
PUBLISHING

Please visit our website, www.garethstevens.com. For a free color catalog of all our high-quality books, call toll free 1-800-542-2595 or fax 1-877-542-2596.

Library of Congress Cataloging-in-Publication Data

Rajczak, Kristen.
 The Shoshone people / Kristen Rajczak.
     pages cm. — (Native American cultures)
 Includes index.
 ISBN 978-1-4824-1994-8 (pbk.)
 ISBN 978-1-4824-1993-1 (6 pack)
 ISBN 978-1-4824-1995-5 (library binding)
 1. Shoshoni Indians—Juvenile literature. I. Title.
 E99.S4R36 2015
 978.004'974574—dc23

                                    2014031943

First Edition

Published in 2015 by
Gareth Stevens Publishing
111 East 14th Street, Suite 349
New York, NY 10003

Copyright © 2015 Gareth Stevens Publishing

Designer: Sarah Liddell
Editor: Therese Shea

Photo credits: Cover, pp. 1 (main, Shoshone warrior, ring and pin game, water canteen), 11, 13, 18, 27, 29 Marilyn Angel Wynn/Nativestock/Getty Images; cover, p. 1 (moccasins) Daderot/Wikimedia Commons; pp. 5, 8, 23 Rainer Lesniewski/Shutterstock.com; p. 7 altrendo nature/Getty Images; p. 9 Rmhermen/Wikimedia Commons; p. 10 Tom Reichner/Shutterstock.com; p. 15 Otto Herschan/Stringer/Getty Images; p. 17 Tungsten/Wikimedia Commons; p. 19 Three Lions/Stringer/Getty Images; p. 21 RHorning/Wikimedia Commons; p. 22 US National Archives/Wikimedia Commons.

Printed in the United States of America

CPSIA compliance information: Batch #CW15GS: For further information contact Gareth Stevens, New York, New York at 1-800-542-2595.

CONTENTS

Words in the glossary appear in **bold** type the first time they are used in the text.

NATIVE PEOPLE

For thousands of years before European explorers reached the Americas, Native American tribes made their homes and found food on the beautiful land that later became the United States. They believed in treating the land with respect and gave thanks for the animals and plants they were able to hunt and gather. The Shoshone (shoh-SHOH-nee) people are one of these many native tribes.

The Shoshone lived in the western half of the present-day United States where California, Utah, Montana, Wyoming, Nevada, Oregon, and Idaho are today.

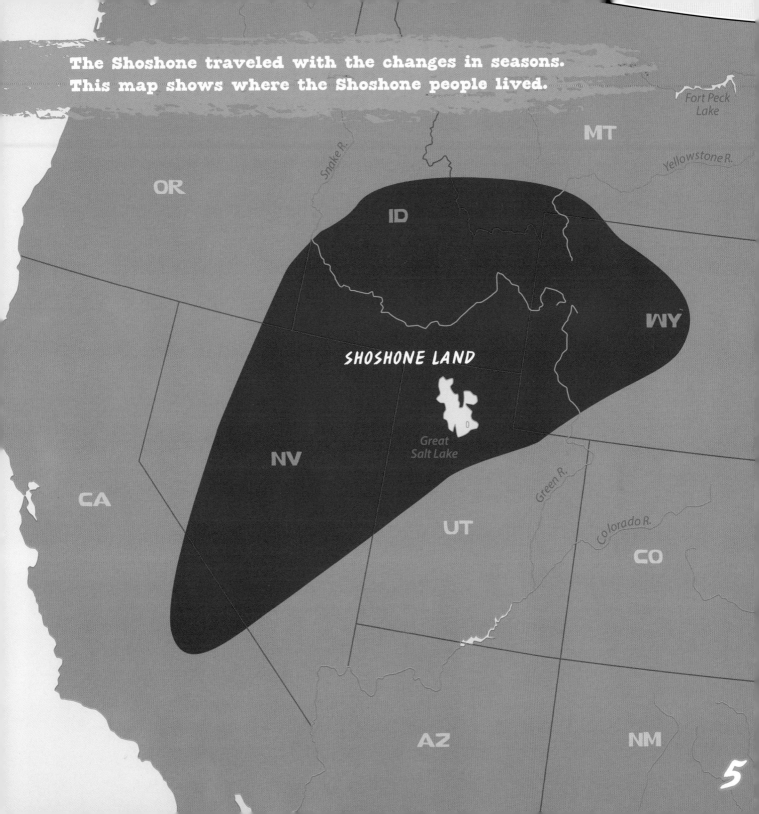

The Shoshone traveled with the changes in seasons. This map shows where the Shoshone people lived.

Fort Peck Lake

MT

Yellowstone R.

OR

Snake R.

ID

WY

SHOSHONE LAND

Great Salt Lake

NV

CA

UT

Green R.

Colorado R.

CO

AZ

NM

CREATING THE SHOSHONE

The Shoshone have stories explaining how they came to be. One tale tells of how Wolf, the creator god, formed Earth. Coyote, his brother, later populated Earth with his sons and daughters. They jumped from a water jug Coyote carried. This explains why different bands of Shoshone people were spread out over a large area.

Scientists know that the **ancestors** of the Shoshone and other Native Americans first settled in North America more than 12,000 years ago. Over thousands of years, different tribes formed and settled in many places.

Ancestors of the Shoshone and Paiute Indians made these carvings in rock in California. Called petroglyphs, similar carvings can be found in historic Shoshone territory and range in age from 5,000 to 200 years old.

7

THE THREE GROUPS

The Shoshone people settled in three main areas. They became the Northern, Eastern, and Western Shoshone.

The Northern Shoshone mostly lived near the Snake River in present-day Idaho and western Wyoming. They fished for salmon and hunted buffalo for food and clothing. The Northern Shoshone made cone-shaped homes, called tepees or tipis, out of buffalo skin. These were fitting homes for the nomadic Shoshone, because they were easy to put up and take down.

MT

SNAKE RIVER

OR

ID

9

BUFFALO AND HORSES

The Eastern Shoshone lived in western Wyoming. They lived in the valleys of Green River and Wind River, in the Rocky Mountains, and near Yellowstone Lake. The Eastern Shoshone are sometimes called the Wind River Shoshone.

Like the Northern Shoshone, the Eastern Shoshone hunted buffalo for food and clothing. These two groups were introduced to horses around the same time, likely during the late 1600s. It changed their way of life. They could get places faster, travel further, and hunt more easily.

BUFFALO

Northern and Eastern Shoshone became skilled buffalo hunters on horseback. In fact, the Northern Shoshone are sometimes called the "horse Shoshone."

WESTERN SHOSHONE

The Western Shoshone were found mostly in present-day Nevada and parts of Utah and California. They're sometimes called the "unmounted" Shoshone. They didn't have as many horses as their relatives to the east and north.

The Western Shoshone lived in huts called wickiups made of bark, branches, and grass. They hunted a little, but mostly ate food they gathered, such as seeds and nuts. They were sometimes called the disrespectful name "Diggers," because they dug in the ground for food such as roots.

DID YOU KNOW?

The Shoshone call themselves Newe (nuh-WUH), which means "the people." "Shoshone" was probably a name given to them by others.

Nomadic Native Americans in the western and southwestern United States often built wickiup homes.

SHOSHONE FAMILIES

The Shoshone people had some practices in common. They traveled in small groups with their families, including aunts, uncles, and grandparents. A few times a year, they would all come together for **celebrations** or hunts.

Shoshone men hunted and, when needed, would fight. Women built the family homes, cooked, and took care of children. Children were allowed to play, but they also gathered food and prepared for the family to move again. They learned skills they'd use later in life, too.

DID YOU KNOW?

The Shoshone wore clothing made from animal skins. Some were decorated with beads or porcupine quills!

Shoshone babies were carried on their mother's back in a carrier called a cradleboard.

In 1804, Meriwether Lewis, William Clark, and a small party set out to explore the lands of the **Louisiana Purchase**. They met a group of Native Americans called the Hidatsa. In the Hidatsa village, they hired a French-Canadian trapper and his wife to be **interpreters** on their journey.

The woman was Sacagawea, a Shoshone who had been taken from her family as a girl to live with the Hidatsa. With Sacagawea's help, Lewis and Clark later were able to get horses from the Shoshone for their journey over the Rocky Mountains.

DID YOU KNOW?

Lewis and Clark were likely the first white men the Shoshone had ever met.

Sacagawea is thought to have been a member of the Wind River Shoshone. She helped Lewis and Clark find their way through her people's territory.

The Western Shoshone first came upon white fur trappers around the late 1820s. By the 1840s, gold was found around their lands. Many settlers were coming to and through their territory trying to strike it rich.

As more people headed west, they began claiming land on which Shoshone lived, hunted, and gathered food. Food became harder to find. As a result, some Shoshone began to steal from settlers and **raid** wagon trains. Fighting between whites and Shoshone increased.

DID YOU KNOW?

The Shoshone used buffalo-skin shields and bows and arrows as weapons.

Settlers began pushing the Shoshone off land the
natives had been living on for many years.

BEAR RIVER MASSACRE

A group of Shoshone, led by Chief Bear Hunter, were some who had attacked settlers in Utah. They thought their land was being stolen. In January 1863, US soldiers attacked back as these Shoshone slept near the modern border between Idaho and Utah. The Shoshone fought back. However, they were greatly outnumbered and outgunned. More than 250 Shoshone were killed, including many women and children.

Today, this event is called the Bear River **Massacre**. It was the largest number of Native American deaths from one attack ever.

DID YOU KNOW?

Between 1863 and 1890, there were six major Native American massacres in the western half of North America.

This monument stands in honor of those who died in the Bear River Massacre.

WIND RIVER RESERVATION

During the second half of the 1800s, Native American tribes were being forced onto land set aside by the US government called reservations. The Shoshone were no different.

The Wind River Reservation was established in 1868 for the Eastern Shoshone. Chief Washakie, their leader, worked peacefully with the government to place the reservation on territory his people had been living on for years. However, the **treaty** Washakie signed was later ignored, and the land promised to the Eastern Shoshone shrank.

CHIEF WASHAKIE

DID YOU KNOW?

After the Bear River Massacre, the Fort Hall Reservation was established in 1868 in Idaho for Shoshone and Bannock native peoples.

Today, the Shoshone share some of their reservations with other Native American groups, such as the Arapaho. The Wind River Reservation is the third-largest reservation in the United States.

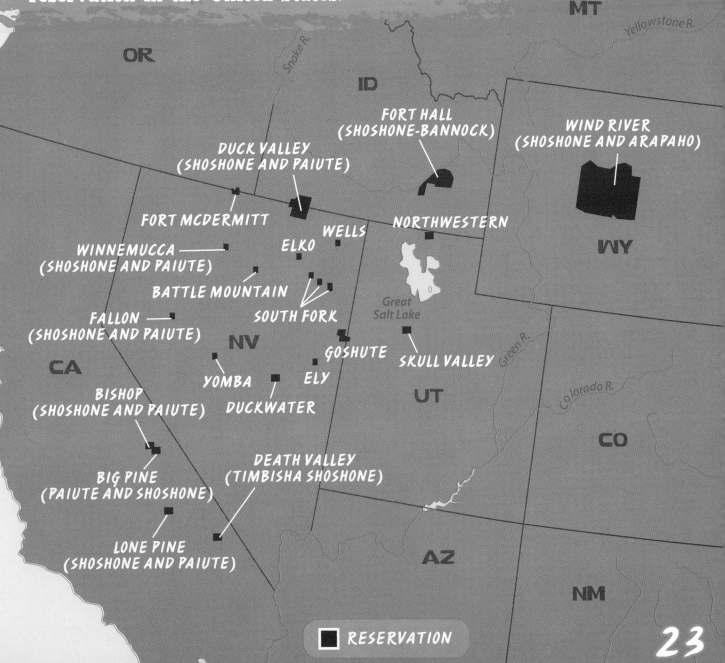

MT

OR

ID

Fort Peck Lake

Yellowstone R.

Snake R.

FORT HALL
(SHOSHONE-BANNOCK)

WIND RIVER
(SHOSHONE AND ARAPAHO)

DUCK VALLEY
(SHOSHONE AND PAIUTE)

FORT MCDERMITT

WELLS

NORTHWESTERN

WY

WINNEMUCCA
(SHOSHONE AND PAIUTE)

ELKO

BATTLE MOUNTAIN

SOUTH FORK

Great Salt Lake

FALLON
(SHOSHONE AND PAIUTE)

NV

Green R.

CA

YOMBA

GOSHUTE

ELY

SKULL VALLEY

Colorado R.

BISHOP
(SHOSHONE AND PAIUTE)

DUCKWATER

UT

CO

BIG PINE
(PAIUTE AND SHOSHONE)

DEATH VALLEY
(TIMBISHA SHOSHONE)

LONE PINE
(SHOSHONE AND PAIUTE)

AZ

NM

☐ RESERVATION

23

LAND LOSS

In 1875, a reservation was founded for the Shoshone of Lemhi Valley in Idaho. After just 30 years, however, they were forced to move. Their hard journey to the Fort Hall Reservation is sometimes called another Trail of Tears.

Some Shoshone in Utah lived peacefully among **Mormon** settlers, who lent them land to farm. However, in 1960, the Mormons decided to sell the farmland, called the Washakie settlement. They burned down Shoshone homes, thinking they were empty. However, many weren't. The Mormons gave them nearby land.

DID YOU KNOW?

The first Trail of Tears was during the 1830s. Around 100,000 Eastern Woodland Indians, including the Cherokee, were forced to leave their land and go west. About 15,000 died on the journey.

SHOSHONE HISTORY

AD 500
Shoshone ancestors form small groups around North America.

1805
Lewis and Clark meet Shoshone people during their exploration of the Louisiana Purchase.

1600s
Eastern and Northern Shoshone are introduced to horses.

1820s
The Western Shoshone begin encountering white fur trappers.

1840s
Gold and land bring settlers into Shoshone territory.

1863
The Bear River Massacre occurs.

1868
The Wind River Reservation is established.

1875
The Lemhi Valley Reservation is established.

1905
The Shoshone Trail of Tears takes place as they move to the Fort Hall Reservation.

SHOSHONE TODAY

There are between 30,000 and 40,000 Shoshone in the United States today. Many live on reservations that have their own government and laws. Most of the nine Shoshone tribes of today no longer have a chief as a leader. Instead, they vote for a group of leaders.

Other Shoshone live in cities and towns across the United States. They're mainly in Idaho, Nevada, Wyoming, Montana, Utah, and California, like their ancestors. Whether on a reservation or not, it's common for Shoshone to celebrate their rich history.

DID YOU KNOW?

Most Shoshone speak English. About 1,000 still speak their native language.

Modern-day Shoshone only dress in decorated
clothing like this for celebrations.

27

RECOGNITION

Today, some Shoshone work as ranchers or farmers. Others have allowed the US government to drill for oil and gas on their land to make money. Shoshone have opened casinos on their land as well.

Some Shoshone tribes aren't federally, or nationally, recognized. Their recognition would be an important step in making others aware of their connections to the history of westward growth in the United States. These Shoshone continue to work toward this goal.

DID YOU KNOW?

Casinos are places where people gamble, or bet money on many kinds of games. They've become a common source of money for Native American tribes.

Shoshone firefighters and their families march in a parade on the Fort Hall Reservation in Idaho.

29

ancestor: a relative who lived long ago

celebration: a time to show happiness for an event through activities such as eating or playing music

interpreter: someone who tells the meaning of another language

Louisiana Purchase: territory of the western United States bought from France in 1803

massacre: the killing of a large number of people, especially when they cannot defend themselves

Mormon: a member of the Church of Jesus Christ of Latter-day Saints, founded in 1830 and centered in Salt Lake City, Utah

quill: a sharp, stiff point on the body of an animal

raid: to attack suddenly

treaty: an agreement between countries or peoples

weapon: something used to cause someone or something injury or death

FOR MORE INFORMATION

BOOKS

De Capua, Sarah. *The Shoshone*. New York, NY: Marshall Cavendish Benchmark, 2008.

Dennis, Yvonne Wakim. *A Kid's Guide to Native American History: More Than 50 Activities*. Chicago, IL: Chicago Review Press, 2010.

Norwich, Grace. *I Am Sacagawea*. New York, NY: Scholastic, Inc., 2012.

WEBSITES

Shoshone Indian Fact Sheet
www.bigorrin.org/shoshone_kids.htm
Learn the answers to many questions about the Shoshone people.

The Shoshone Indians
shoshoneindian.com
Read about many parts of Shoshone culture, including history and famous people.

INDEX